ART IN NATURE

EMILY KINGTON

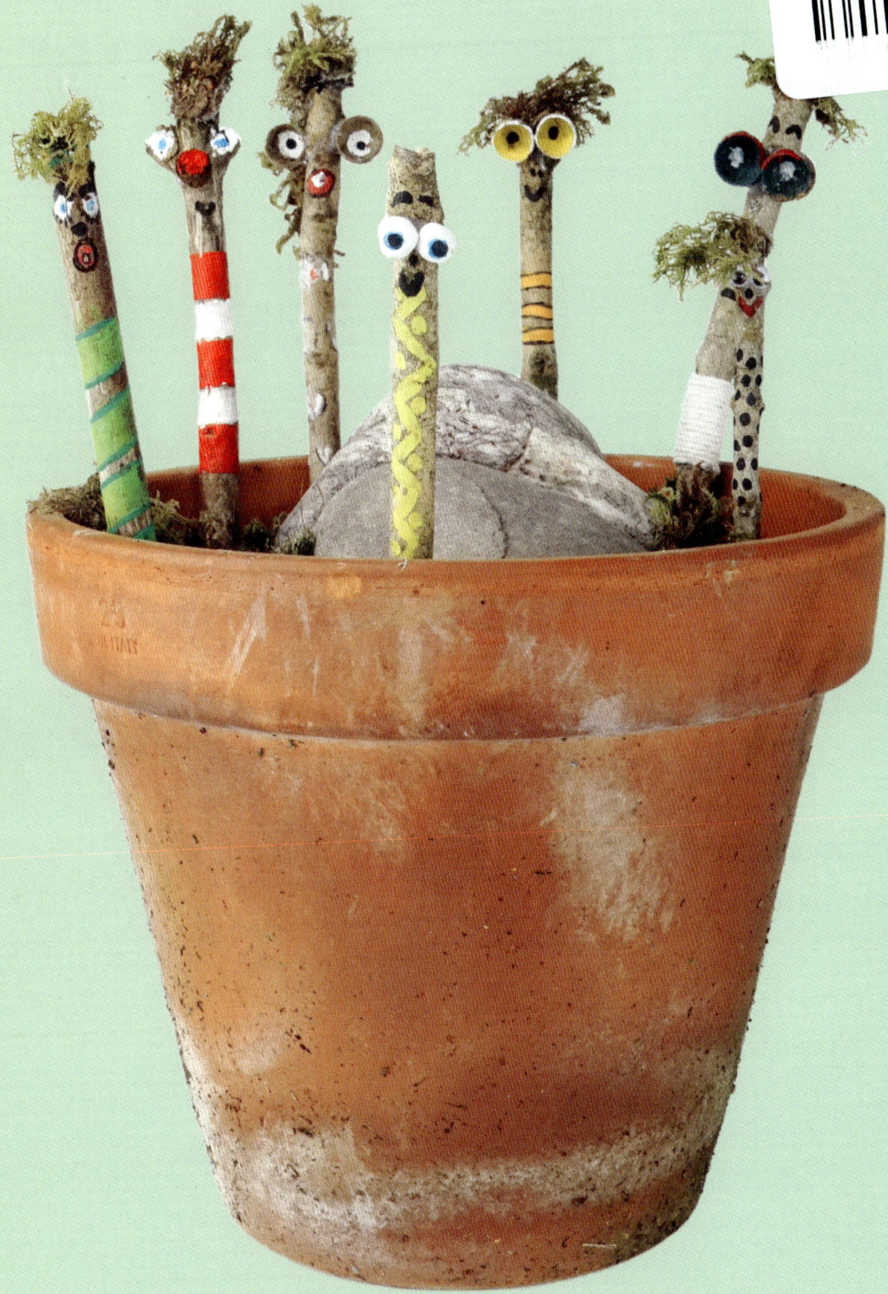

CONTENTS

It's great fun getting outside and exploring the world around you. There are so many things to do and see in nature, all year long. Here are some fantastic things to build or make from things you can find when you're out and about.

Get your wellies on and go out on a nature hunt. Turn the page to discover some of the things you need to find to make the fun crafts in this book...

NATURE HUNT CHALLENGE — 4

LONG-NECKED DINOSAUR — 6

FUNNY STICK MONSTERS — 8

PEBBLE PEOPLE — 10

SHIP AHOY! — 12

PEBBLE ART — 16

NEED HELP?
Watch out for this sign throughout the book. You may need help from an adult when completing these tasks.

BUILD A WOOD STACK  18

LEAF GALLERY 20

MINI NATURE CAMP 22

TAKE CARE OUT AND ABOUT  24

NATURE HUNT CHALLENGE

For some of these projects, you will need to take time out and go on a nature hunt!

NATURE HUNT SAFETY

Never go out into nature alone; make sure to always go with an adult and stay together to keep safe. It can be easy to get distracted but be careful not to get separated.

Beware, some bugs can be poisonous and may bite.

Always wash your hands after handling bugs or soil.

TAKING CARE OF THE ENVIRONMENT

Only collect nature finds from the ground. Don't pick anything off trees or plants like branches or leaves as that will damage the plant.

Treat insects with care and don't forget to release them.

LEAVES

These can be found on fallen branches or the ground. How many different shape and size leaves can you find?

STONES AND PEBBLES

Look for different shapes - flat, round or unusual - as well as different sizes and colours.

STICKS

Always be on the lookout for sticks of all different sizes.

MOSS

Moss often grows in woods, on fallen branches or on the floor. Only take a little from an area where there is already a lot.

ALL SORTS

Pine cones, acorns and seeds.

VINES

Vine stems are strong and can be used to hold things together.

MUD, MARVELLOUS MUD!

Lovely sticky mud – the stickier the better. A good alternative would be paper clay.

WOOD

Collect interesting pieces of wood.

BARK

Look for fallen branches and loose bark.

YOU WILL ALSO NEED:

- Gloves
- Wellington boots
- Old bag or box (to carry items home)
- Small trowel/old spoon (for collecting mud)
- Paper clay
- Pencil
- Pencil sharpener
- Felt tip pens
- Acrylic paint
- Paintbrushes
- String
- Strong glue
- Scissors (but don't use these without an adult)
- Soap or washing up liquid
- A bowl
- An old plant pot

LONG-NECKED DINOSAUR

Find some old bark to make this cool creature! Make sure you wear gloves when handling bark and sticks to protect your hands.

YOU WILL NEED:

- Good-sized clump of mud
- Various pieces of bark
- 4 sticks, all similar length
- Acrylic paint
- Paintbrush
- Strong glue

1. Use the clump of mud for the base, then push in the four sticks for the dinosaur legs.

2. Collect lots of different shaped pieces of bark. These will be used to create your dinosaur.

The body has been made from several pieces of bark glued together.

3. Break bark into pieces like this for the tail, body and neck/head.

Use the longest pieces for the neck and tail.

The bottom jaw can be painted red and glued onto the head, then paint on the eyes.

4. Glue the body to the top of the legs and then glue on the tail and neck/head.

THIS DINOSAUR IS SO COOL, YOU CAN ALMOST HEAR IT ROAR!

FUNNY STICK MONSTERS

Make some funny stick monsters. Stick them in a pot or hide them in your garden.

YOU WILL NEED:

- Small sticks
- Moss
- Seeds or acorn tops
- Sticky mud
- Old plant pot
- Big stone
- Acrylic paint
- Paintbrushes
- Strong glue (if your mud isn't sticky enough!)

TOP TIP

If your monsters aren't standing up straight in their pot, add a little glue to help them. Don't use glue in the garden - find mud or soil that will help them stand up.

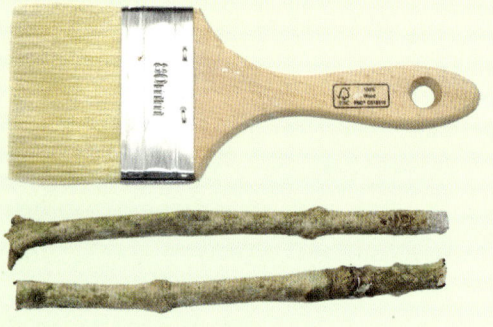

1. Clean the surface of the sticks with a brush, ready to paint.

2. Paint each stick in different colours. Get creative with shapes and patterns.

Add some moss to create a wild monster hairdo!

3. Add some whacky features, like eyes and hair, using seeds, acorn tops and moss.

4. If you are using a plant pot to display your monsters, fill it with mud and cover with a layer of moss.

Add a big stone for the monsters to stand around.

5. Arrange your monster stick friends into a really cool sculpture – somewhere in your garden!

PEBBLE PEOPLE

You can make quite impressive pictures using pebbles and stones. It's easy for small hands to do, too!

YOU WILL NEED:

- Pebbles and stones (different shape, sizes and colours)
- Sticky mud
- A large piece of wood
- Lots of stems from leaves or vines
- Soap or washing up liquid
- Water
- A bowl
- Paintbrush
- Felt tip pen

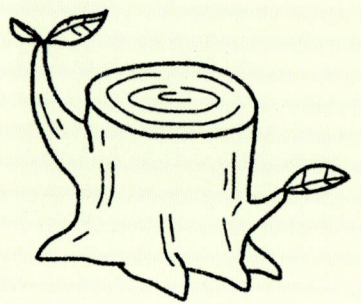

1. Wash all of your pebbles and stones in warm, soapy water. Leave them to dry.

2. Use a brush to clean the surface of the wood. This will be the base.

3. Spend some time arranging the stones into different-shaped people and set them aside.

Add happy faces to some of the pebbles!

4. Spread a thick layer of mud onto your wooden base.

The mud needs to be thick enough to push the stones into.

Use stems from leaves or vines for the sunrays.

5. Push the stone people into the mud and repeat the process to add the Sun.

HERE ARE SOME PEBBLE FRIENDS ENJOYING THE SUNSET!

11

SHIP AHOY!

You can make this pirate ship, and a pirate who can sail it away, in no time at all!

YOU WILL NEED:

- A dry piece of bark
- Sticky mud or paper clay
- 2 large leaves
- Moss
- 1 tall stick for the mast
- 1 small stick for the pirate
- Acrylic paint
- Paintbrushes
- Scissors
- Strong glue

1. Use a piece of bark that has a curved shape to it (see step 4).

This is the front of the boat.

2. Lie your bark flat on a surface. Place one portion of sticky mud in the middle and one towards the front. If you don't have mud, use paper clay.

You could even add moss for hair.

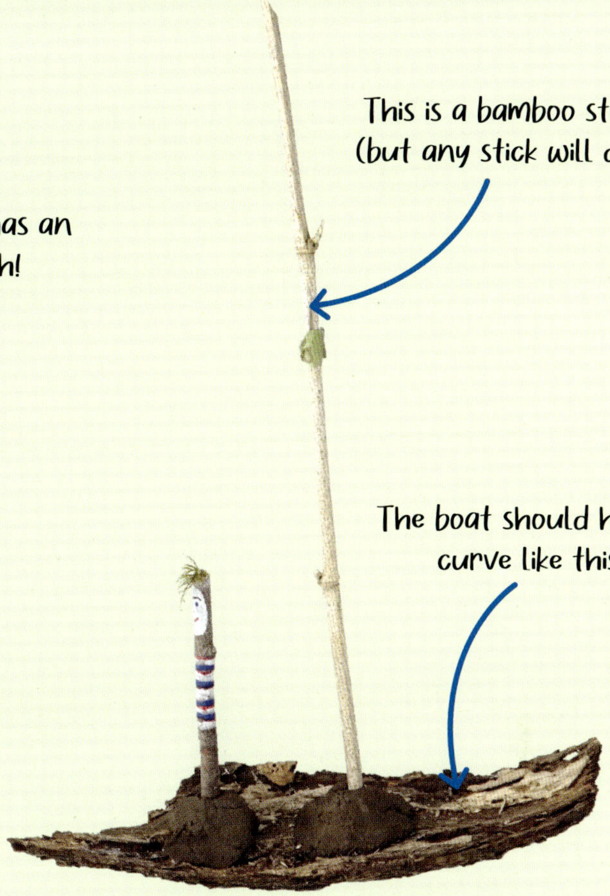

This pirate has an eye-patch!

This is a bamboo stick (but any stick will do).

The boat should have a curve like this.

3. Make a pirate! Paint a face and T-shirt onto a small stick.

4. Push a long, straight stick into the mud in the middle and push the pirate into the mud at the front.

5. Ask an adult to help you trim the leaves to make one large and one small sail.

6. Cut small holes into the leaves and slide them onto the mast stick. You may need to use a dab of glue to hold them in place.

YOUR FINISHED PIRATE SHIP IS READY TO LAUNCH!

THIS SHIP IS READY TO SAIL INTO ITS VERY OWN PIRATE ADVENTURE!

PEBBLE ART

Here is a chance to paint your favourite bugs or animals, and hide them for people to find and admire. Search carefully to find the best stones to use!

YOU WILL NEED:

- Smooth stones and pebbles of different shapes, sizes and colours
- Animal-shaped stones (much harder to find)
- Pencil
- Pencil sharpener
- Acrylic paint or felt tip pens
- Paintbrush
- A bowl
- Soap or washing up liquid
- Water
- A box or bag to store and carry your stones in

1. Wash all of your stones and pebbles in warm, soapy water. Leave them to dry.

2. Draw the outline of bugs or animals in pencil on each of your chosen stones.

3. Carefully colour in your drawings using felt tip pens or paint. Leave them to dry. Then store them ready for your next nature hunt.

4. On your next nature hunt or walk with nature, hide your stones in secret places.

WILL YOU REMEMBER WHERE YOU HID YOUR STONES? REVISIT YOUR HIDING SPOTS LATER TO SEE IF THEY'RE STILL THERE!

Hidden amongst tree roots.

In and around rocks and moss.

In old tree stumps and branches.

BUILD A WOOD STACK

You probably need to go on a woodland walk to build a full-size wood stack. However, anyone can make this mini-version – it can be any size you like!

YOU WILL NEED:
- Lots of straight sticks or branches
- Sticky mud
- Glue (for a mini model)

TOP TIP
This mini wood stack is made from about 25 sticks. A full-size stack would need more than 40 small branches!

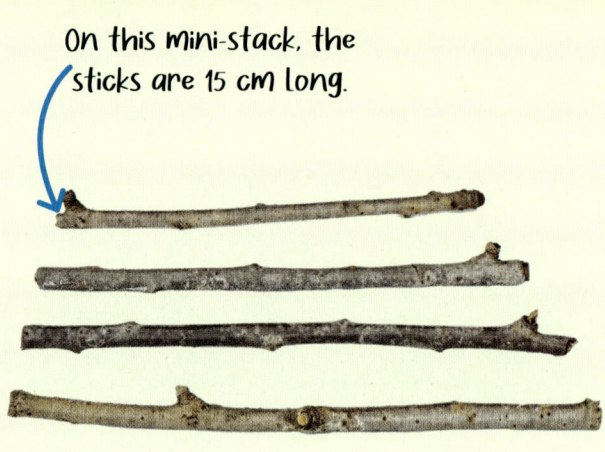

On this mini-stack, the sticks are 15 cm long.

1. Find a good place to build your wood stack where there are lots of sticks or branches around.

2. Decide how big you want your stack to be. The bottom layer will need to be made from your longest sticks or branches.

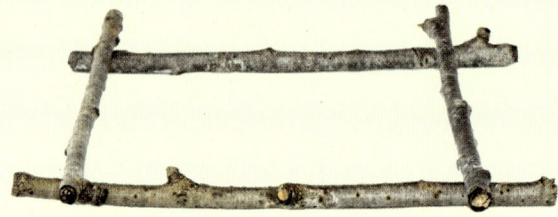

3. You need four sticks the same length for each layer. Place one pair at right angles on top of the other pair, leave a little space at each end. Use sticky mud or glue to hold in place.

4. You will need slightly shorter sticks for each of the next layers. Build the layers up two pairs at a time, each one smaller than the last.

5. Keep adding sticks - your wood stack is almost finished!

6. To finish, use one tiny stick for the final layer.

Quite a feat of engineering!

You can build it big without using the mud, but it may not last as long.

NOW YOU KNOW HOW TO BUILD A SMALL STACK, WHY NOT BUILD A BIG ONE!

19

LEAF GALLERY

Bring art and nature inside with this beautiful leaf display.

YOU WILL NEED:

- 4 sticks of equal length
- Small leaves of different shapes and sizes
- Vine stems
- Stiff brush
- Thick paper or card
- Strong glue
- Acrylic paint or felt tip pens
- String
- Paper towel

1. Clean the sticks with the stiff brush to remove any dirt or old bark. Select some long, strong-looking vines and remove some of the leaves.

2. To make a square frame, lay out the four sticks on a flat surface, placing their ends over each other at right angles as shown.

3. Glue the sticks where they meet to stick them together. To make your frame even stronger, bind the joints together with string. You may need to ask for help to do this.

4. Lay your vines equal distance apart and glue them to the frame as shown.

Make fun shapes, like animals, by arranging different leaves together!

5. Tear pieces of thick paper or card into irregular shapes.

6. Choose your favourite leaves. Carefully wipe them clean with some paper towel to remove any dirt. Then stick the leaves onto the paper or card with glue.

7. Arrange your leaf papers over the frame to decide how you would like it to look. When you're happy with your design, glue the back of the paper to the vines. Ask an adult to help you - you don't want to accidentally stick your gallery to anything else!

MINI NATURE CAMP

This is a perfect mini-camp for your toys to live in. Put it in your garden, on a balcony or even in your bedroom!

YOU WILL NEED:

- 3 strong sticks (for example bamboo)
- Lots of thin sticks
- Moss
- Leaves
- Vines or string

TOP TIP

If you don't have a garden, build your nature camp indoors, using a thick piece of cardboard as a base.

1. Find a flat surface on soft ground; in the shade would be best. Put down a layer of moss for the base.

2. Make a tripod with the three strong sticks, then bind it at the top with vines or string. You may need some help doing this! Then, push the bottom three points into the moss.

3. Layer sticks all around the sides and back of the tripod. These sticks need to be longer than the tripod.

4. Cover the sticks with vines and leaves to make the camp dark and sheltered inside. But make sure to leave one side clear - this will be the entrance.

YOU COULD MAKE A FULL-SIZE CAMP LIKE THIS NEXT TIME YOU GO TO THE WOODS!

TAKE CARE OUT AND ABOUT

It's always brilliant fun when you are out exploring and gathering, but it's a good idea to take some things with you to stay safe.

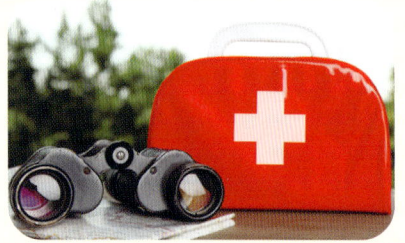

WATER
Take plenty of water. It's easy to become dehydrated in active play.

FIRST AID KIT
Take along a basic first aid kit to deal with scratches and insect bites.

CLOTHING
Wear appropriate clothing and footwear. It can be slippery and wet in woody areas.

SAFETY FIRST

- Never eat any part of a plant or fungus or drink water from a stream.
- Climbing is fun and a real achievement, but check with adults before climbing anything and make sure they stay around to help you. It's not safe to climb alone.
- Beware of dangerous or poisonous wild plants and animals (applicable in some areas).
- Be careful near water. It can often be deeper than it looks.

ALWAYS ASK AN ADULT BEFORE YOU DO ANY OF THE PROJECTS IN THIS BOOK!

Copyright © 2024 Hungry Tomato Ltd

First published in 2024 by Hungry Tomato Ltd
F15, Old Bakery Studios, Blewetts Wharf, Malpas Road, Truro, Cornwall, TR1 1QH, UK.

No part of this publication may be reproduced, stored in a retrieval system, or transmitted in any form or by any means, electronic, mechanical, photocopying, recording, or otherwise, without prior written permission of the copyright owner.

A CIP catalogue record for this book is available from the British Library.

ISBN 9781835693551

Printed in China

Discover more at www.hungrytomato.com

Picture credits:
Abbreviations: m-middle, t-top, l-left, r-right, bg-background.

Aleksey Matrenin 3br; Amorn Suriyan 24tl; Barbadoss 22tl; Evgeny Atamanenko 24tr; Hchjjl 10tr, 20tr, 22tr, (warning sign used throughout); Ilyafs 14-15 bg; Jacob Lund 2tl; LedyX 2tm; Lilac 3bl; Studio KIWI 24tm.

Every effort has been made to trace the copyright holders, and we apologise in advance for any unintentional omissions. We would be pleased to insert the appropriate acknowledgements in any subsequent edition of this publication.